PEARLS TO GO...

YOLANDA FORD-MITCHELL

Copyright

©2017 Yolanda Ford-Mitchell

All rights reserved.

This book is protected under the copyright laws of the United States of America. This book may not be copied or reprinted for commercial gain or profit. The use of short quotations or occasional page copying for personal or group study is permitted and encouraged. Permission will be granted upon request. Unless otherwise identified, Scripture quotations are from English Standard Version (ESV), King James Version of the Bible (KJV), New American Standard version of the Bible (NASB), New King James Version (NKJV), New Living Translation (NLT), Message Version (MSG), Modern English Version (MEV) emphasis within scripture quotes is the author's own.

ISBN 13 9780692978221

For Worldwide Distribution

Printed in the U.S.A.

PREFACE

PEARLS TO GO are short prayers to God that allow the reader and author to agree-"Again, truly I tell you that if two of you on earth agree about anything they ask for, it will be done for them by My Father in heaven." (Matthew 18:19-NIV) The reader is encouraged through prayer to continue a daily walk of passionate devotion to the Lord. The author's focus is to acknowledge points that need to be addressed day-by-day in the believers' prayer life.

This 31-Day Devotional is created to encourage the believer to stir up the spirit of intercession that one uses often when praying for others. The devotional is for you, the reader, to focus on the uplifting of the inner man within your spirit. Today, I pray that when you read this book, it will unleash within you another level of circadian meditation in the Word of God. The prayers were derived from the Holy Scriptures and were compiled by this Christian, who is moving forward in her care for others.

May this book of inspiration bless you and encourage you to go into a deeper level of study and contemplation in God's Word. May you also be motivated to share, and bless someone else with this book.

Peace & Blessings

SPECIAL THANKS TO:

Thank You, GOD, for allowing this book to be presented.

Reverend Wendie G. Howlett-Trott for your gift of love in editing this book.

My Amazing Husband Bernard Mitchell

My Loving Father and Mother: Richard & Alberta Ford-Kennedy

My Siblings: Derrick, Nasheemah, Shanti and Shaquana

All of my Sisters & Brothers in Love and Family

(Boley's, Chamber's, Ferguson's, Ford's, Harley's, Houston's, Kennedy's, Mallard's)

Dr. Virginia Booth

Bishop Dr. Carlton T. Brown & Pastor Lorna I. Brown

Pastors Gary & Mia Carswell

Bishop James G. Rodges & Dr. Phyllis Rodges

TABLE OF CONTENTS

Repentance 1

No Distractions 4

Self Awareness 7

Give God Your Concerns 10

You Are Valuable 13

Let God Lead 16

Balance and Humility Are Necessary 19

Push, Press And Pursue 22

No More Fear 25

Ask God For Wisdom 28

Don't Retaliate 31

Did You Get Your Answer? 34

Stay Focus 37

Thankful 40

What's New? 43

Trust And Obey 46

What's The Truth? 49

Integrity 52

Compassion Within You 55

Do You Delegate Or Multitask? 58

Being Content 61

Forgiveness 64

Is Your Lamp Lit? 67

Be Encouraged 70

Temptation Is Not From God 73

During The Test 76

Check Your Motives 79

Faith And Works 82

Fruit Of Your Lips 85

Joyous Laughter 88

What's Your Contribution? 91

DAY 1

Repentance

Today, I pray that you enjoy your daily installment in spending time with God, and that He calls you by His name. You are considering how good He has been, and you are so grateful that you have the opportunity to communicate with Him. You know that prayer is important—a vital necessity—along with reading the Holy Scriptures for guidance. We want God to be merciful and gracious to us, and if we have dishonored Him in any way we want to sincerely repent. We want God to answer our prayers in a favorable way, and to feel His presence and His love.

PEARL NOTE

"Then if My people who are called by My name will humble themselves and pray and seek My face and turn from their wicked ways, I will hear from heaven and will forgive their sins and restore their land."

2 Chronicles 7:14 (NLT)

DAY 2

No Distractions

Today, I pray that the peace of God will rest in your mind; that you will stay in tune with the thoughts of God. The distractions that have been assigned to draw your attention from the things of God are no longer effective. The peace of God will give you clarity in your vision and your perception will be clear to focus on the matters that God has assigned to you; that you may articulate the heart of God with precision and power; that someone would come to know Jesus Christ as their Lord and Savior. I declare that the will of God is the priority of your life; and today you will bless those around you! I decree and declare these things in Jesus' Name.

PEARL NOTE

"Do not be conformed to this world, but be transformed by the renewing of your mind, that you may prove what is the good and acceptable and perfect will of God."

Romans 12:2 (MEV)

DAY 3

Self Awareness

Today, I pray that you will look at yourself as useful to the Kingdom of God. I pray that you are encouraged by the plans that God has for you. See yourself strategically placed and purposeful in attending to the assignment that you have been called to do, with a merry heart and joyful speech, and with a countenance that illuminates the place that God has chosen for you. You have Joy, Peace and Love! As you work with the intent to please your Father, your strength is evident. Although there will be challenges, you will overcome them and will not give up or be replaced. The work that you do for the Lord is necessary In Jesus' Name.

PEARL NOTE

"Therefore, my beloved brethren, be ye steadfast, unmovable, always abounding in the work of the Lord, forasmuch as ye know that your labor in not in vain in the Lord."

1 Corinthians 15:58 (KJV)

DAY 4

Give God Your Concerns

Today, I pray that you cast your worries, frustrations and concerns upon the Lord, knowing that the work He began He will also complete. He promised to never leave you or forsake you; so you can rest in Him. He has traveled with you through storms and calm seas. Believe that He will be with you until the end of time. The load that you carry is not for you. So, give it to the One that will bear the burden for us all. He wants you free to rejoice in Him. Today, you will hand over the things that are weighty and unnecessary to carry in order to travel lightly into His marvelous light. In Jesus' Name.

PEARL NOTE

"Are you tired? Worn out? Burned out on religion? Come to Me. Get away with Me and you will recover your life. I will show you how to take a real rest. Walk with Me; work with Me—watch how I do it. Learn the unforced rhythms of grace. I won't lay anything heavy or ill-fitting on you. Keep company with Me and you will learn to live freely and lightly."

Matthew 11: 28-30 (MSG)

DAY 5

You Are Valuable

Today, I pray that you will consider your surroundings, and all that belongs to you. Today you will confirm, with the heavenlies, that God has given you power to tread on the wicked things that plan to sneak into your destiny and mask your purpose. The source of wickedness has no legal access to your destiny. You have been given authority to praise and worship and to create the atmosphere for welcoming the presence of God. He has ordained you to worship Him. The atmosphere will be set to glorify your Father for all He has done for you. You are comforted in His presence by the worship. You have been given the authority to confess that you were created in the very likeness of God and are His workmanship! In Jesus' Name.

PEARL NOTE

"I have given you authority to trample on snakes and scorpions and to overcome all the power of the enemy; nothing will harm you."

Luke 10:19 (NIV)

DAY 6

Let God Lead

Today, I pray you have confidence in knowing that you are led of the Lord, and that you trust that He understands all things. He is Master of all plans and has you in mind. Your relationship keeps you communicating with Him about everything. He is so happy to hear from you, and He positions you as you rely on Him for direction. Your posture is upright when your dependency is on Him. He shows you a path that your thoughts alone could not travel. Yes! He is guiding you into His Divine direction for your life: and those around you will be the beneficiaries of your journey. In Jesus' Name.

PEARL NOTE

"Trust in the Lord with all your heart, and lean not on your own understanding; in all your ways acknowledge Him, and He will direct your path."

Proverbs 3: 5-7 (NIV)

DAY 7

Balance and Humility Are Necessary

Today, I pray that you are balanced with the accomplishments of this world, and the gifts of God that have been created in you. Your desire to seek after the things of God will be valued by you. The more the world desires to magnify your success, the more you will desire to look for validation from your Father; and He will guide and protect you in your most vulnerable places. So, the bait of Satan will not be a snare for your feet. There are many things that you can boast about… But, the humility of your salvation will be recognized as you show compassion to others, understanding that the Grace of God has been a present help in the time of trouble. All the earthly treasures a person could receive have no value in the light of the precious gift of being saved by Him. So, acknowledge today that the importance of your salvation can never be compared to the profits of this world. In Jesus' Name.

PEARL NOTE

_____

_____

_____

_____

_____

_____

_____

_____

_____

_____

"For what shall it profit man, if he gain the whole world, and lose his own soul?"

Mark 8:36 (KJV)

DAY 8

Push, Press And Pursue

Today, I pray that you will continue to walk in your calling, even in the hard places. You will find resilience to pursue. The bigger picture is motivating you, and your understanding is expanding to higher heights and deeper depths. You have claimed heaven as your home. However, the call will be fulfilled as you push, press and pursue. You are traveling to greater places in God, and it's all according to His plan. It is not easy. But, the prize is attainable. Your present viewpoint may not give you the impression that this can be done. However, hope and belief will accelerate your vision beyond the natural. In Jesus' Name.

PEARL NOTE

"I press on toward the goal for the prize of the upward call of God in Christ Jesus."

Philippians 3:14 (NASB)

DAY 9

No More Fear

Today, I pray that fear will no longer grip and engage with your passion to move forward. Your thoughts will not consume you with hopeless possibilities. The fear that once had power over you has no effect on the purpose of your life. Your level of faith now silences your fear(s) and you follow the path of righteousness for His name's sake. The faith you exhibit brings forth a light that brightens the path of the journey, and highlights the effect of courage in the place yet unseen. The mind is tuned in to the instructions of the Holy Spirit and it flows without hesitation. Fear, you have no place here! In Jesus' Name.

PEARL NOTE

"For God hath not given us the spirit of fear, but of power, and love and of a sound mind."

2 Timothy 1:7 (KJV

DAY 10

Ask God For Wisdom

Today, I pray that you seek wisdom to lead and guide others, and to express the thoughts that come from within. Your ability to articulate and express amazing knowledge to others is without question. Remember that the wisdom of God cannot be duplicated for it has untraceable timing, and comes solely from Him. Call and ask Him for His wisdom and He will deliver it upon request. The Holy Spirit will supply the wisdom of God to your spirit, and His advice to you will be taken seriously. For it is God's wisdom that, keeps us from the destruction of this world and prevents us from playing the role of the fool. When wisdom is utilized, folly has no purpose. In Jesus' Name.

PEARL NOTE

"For the Lord gives wisdom; out of His mouth come knowledge and understanding. He lays up sound wisdom for the righteous."

Proverbs 2:6 (MEV)

DAY 11

Don't Retaliate

Today, I pray that you will stand firm in the Lord, and that you will be known for weathering and conquering opposition. You may feel that you should take action. However, this is an opportunity to see the whole picture. The opposition or maybe the lie that the enemy uttered against you, makes you take a closer look into what God says concerning you. You stand in knowing that every word that God says about you is true. You have victory in this area, and you have chosen to stand in truth and purpose. Your flag of surrender to the will of God allows Him to take the battle into His own hands. The angels are in position to assume the direction in which you send them. There is not one finger needed for His vengeance to be unleashed; yet, we still cry: Lord have mercy! In Jesus' Name.

PEARL NOTE

"Dear friends, never take revenge. Leave that to the righteous anger of God. For the Scriptures say, 'I will take revenge; I will pay them back,' says the Lord."

Romans 12:19 (NLT)

DAY 12

Did You Get Your Answer?

Today, I pray that you will have a talk with God concerning matters that are on your heart, and discuss your needs and your heart's desires required to fulfill your kingdom assignment, as a righteous child of God. God is your Source and Supplier of all things; so, you'll have this discussion with Him, and He will respond with specificity, concerning the agenda He has set for you. Your responsibility is to put Him first. He is the first to hear your request and He is the first to release His response. He is the first to decide what you need, and He is the first to create the agenda for your plan. When He is the first, everything that He has stored up for you will be released. I declare you will have relief in knowing His decision for your life, and His ability to give you what you need! There is no need to worry! In Jesus' Name.

PEARL NOTE

"For after all these things the Gentiles seek. For your heavenly Father knows that you need all these things. But seek first the Kingdom of God and His righteousness, and all these things shall be added to you. Therefore, do not worry about tomorrow, for tomorrow will worry about its own things. Sufficient for the day is its own trouble."

Matthew 6:32 -34 (MSG)

DAY 13

Stay Focus

Today, I pray that your gaze will intensify to help you focus on the place where you are now. The plan for you has already been established by God, and placed–within you is purpose and all tools necessary for you to complete the task at hand. Why? Because your help comes from God, and you are traveling with your eyes fixed on Him. As you look beyond your circumstances and present obstacles, you are being strengthened beyond your normal reach. The strength that He provides is flawless; for it supersedes the natural strength of mere man, and brings assurances that propel your momentum forward. It reaches beyond the skies of the earth. Your focus helps pull you up beyond the status quo. I declare that you are the winner in this obstacle course, because your eyes are on the prize and your feet are standing on the Word of God. In Jesus' Name.

PEARL NOTE

"*I look up to the mountains; does my strength come from mountains? No, my strength comes from* GOD, *who made heaven, and earth, and mountains. He won't let you stumble; your Guardian God won't fall asleep. Not on your life! Israel's Guardian will never doze or sleep.*"

Psalm 121: 1-4 (MSG)

DAY 14

Thankful

Today, I pray that you will give thanks and gratitude to God who deserves the glory. You will look at the places that were difficult and recognize that it was Him. You will not only glorify Him to Him -you will find someone to testify of the goodness and faithfulness of God that you have witnessed in your life. There are two things that God can be glorified for immediately: He woke you up this day and you are in your right mind as you read this page.

Can you think of something He has done in your life that you thought was impossible? So, today you can honestly testify that He handled your situation, and because of Him the victory is now yours!

PEARL NOTE

"Give thanks to the Lord, call on His name; make known His deeds among the peoples."

1 Chronicles 16:8 (KJV)

DAY 15

What's New?

Today, I pray that you discover the new thing that God is calling you to do. We know there is nothing new under the sun in the eyes of God. However, there is something that you have never done before in your entire life; or perhaps you have done it before, but have never done it this way. Well, God is calling you to a new thing. Entering into something new means: getting rid of something old and having a moment of introduction to the new thing. The period of introduction is utilized to allow God to create your team and know your strengths as well as your weaknesses. The new thing that you encounter you will be prepared for, and the team that God has created for you will be well balanced… the cream of the crop! In Jesus' Name.

PEARL NOTE

"Do not remember the former things nor consider the things of old. See, I will do a new thing, now it shall spring forth; shall you not be aware of it?"

Isaiah 43:18-19 (KJV)

DAY 16

Trust And Obey

Today, I pray that you will consider your faith walk. The itinerary is based on God's command for you to trust Him. Obedience is the key you must hold in order to enter the place to which He has called you. The practice of obedience shows that we trust in Him—The One in whom we believe. How is your trust? Faith ushers in the fullness of God, and it pleases Him to know that you are trusting His direction without knowing where you are going! Abraham, who is the Father of faith, is our example, as we process our walk of faith. He was an imperfect man, with promises from God, who because of delay in the arrival of a child, entertained an intervention of his own. Yet, God kept His promise to him. You shall see God's faithfulness towards you, and you will trust and obey Him in areas you could have never imagined! All this will be done peacefully! In Jesus' Name.

PEARL NOTE

"By faith Abraham, when he was called by God], obeyed by going to a place which he was to receive as an inheritance; and he went, not knowing where he was going."

Hebrews 11:8 (AMP)

DAY 17

What's The Truth?

Today, I pray that you confront the things that are not true about you; that you have accepted and ask God to reveal those lies that are stumbling blocks in your life. So, you can address them to receive the best. The truth is important to getting you and keeping you in alignment with God; although the truth of inadequacies can be painful! It is necessary that we are truthful about the areas with which we need help. We are created to live in liberty. The desire to live a lie keeps us from a place of liberation and abundance. The truth is accurate, honest, valid and factual and it shapes the reality of your life. The truth takes you right to the freedom that God has ordained for you; it will be well with you in your mission to help others find a place of freedom. Enjoy your truthful and liberating place! In Jesus' Name.

PEARL NOTE

"And you shall know the truth and the truth shall make you free."

John 8: 32 (NKJV)

DAY 18

Integrity

Today, I pray that you have a desire to do everything the right way with no harmful shortcuts knowing that everything done will be pleasing to God. The opportunities that come your way--with compromise--you will resist! You will approach every endeavor reverently, and present them to the Lord for His approval. There may be some things that you feel are not progressing or developing, or that once looked like a *"God Thing"* but now you have discovered they are instead just a *"Good Thing"*. But, God was not invited to participate with you in the "Good Thing", you must now go back and ask God to guide you with integrity, so that the endeavors will be subject to His changes for His honor and glory. Uprightness is desired by man, but MUST be guided by God. If your deepest desire is to be guided by God to do it right, He will show you how. In Jesus' Name.

PEARL NOTE

"The integrity of the upright guides them, but the unfaithful are destroyed by the duplicity."

Proverbs11:3 (NIV)

DAY 19

Compassion Within You

Today, I pray that you consider the fact that you are a loved, devoted vessel of God; and within you is true compassion. You are forgiving, and compliant, without pride, in spite of personal troubles you have had to endure. You are genuinely concerned about someone else. Trials that you have experienced have made you kind and not bitter. You exude compassion, kindness, and humility; and God has given you amazing perseverance! Your thoughts are merciful, and not vengeful, even when it may appear that vengeance would be the just response. Your process has helped you to be a blessing. In Jesus' Name.

PEARL NOTE

"Put on therefore, as the elect of God, holy and beloved, bowels of mercies, kindness, humbleness of mind, meekness, longsuffering."

Colossians 3:12 (KJV)

DAY 20

Do You Delegate Or Multitask?

Today, I pray that no matter what the circumstance: don't be overwhelmed! You have been assigned to be a multitasker. You have the ability to do this because, you are not relying on your own guidance. You may look at your plate and realize that the tasks are not all yours. Wisely, you may have to delegate some responsibilities to others, or even decide whether or not all of the obligations set before you are even meant for you to address.

Rather, it's completing the multiple tasks or the delegation of the tasks to others that God has chosen to come along side you. Your strength is not your own. May the Lord truly strengthen you and guide you in your decision! In Jesus' Name.

PEARL NOTE

"Let the wise listen and add to their learning, and let the discerning get guidance."

Proverbs 1:5 (NIV)

DAY 21

Being Content

Today, I pray that whatever you stand in need of will not be a distraction. God will meet your needs in His time. If you have to wait, please don't be discouraged. It is worth the wait to allow Him to put you at ease in your current place. This ease will allow you to take the limits off of God, and an accept the moves HE chooses to make. There is a time to be at ease, no matter how it looks. God is your source! Talk to Him about being consistent in your contentment. No matter the situation, I declare that you will be content! In Jesus' Name.

PEARL NOTE

"Not that I am speaking of being in need, for I have learned in whatever situation *I am to be content.*"

Philippians 4:11 (ESV)

DAY 22

Forgiveness

Today, I pray that you will forgive, and forgive, and forgive people, and will push past situations that may have caused you to feel disappointment and even fury, to the point that your emotions are out of control. You may have felt vengeful toward others, and even upset with God. Know that you can enter into a place of prayer that will calm you. The forgiveness is a release from the burden of holding on to how you felt when you were wronged. Instead of being angry, show kindness, and be sensitive in knowing that we all make mistakes. Let it go! God forgave you and you will forgive others. In Jesus' Name.

PEARL NOTE

"*Let all bitterness, wrath, anger, outbursts, and blasphemies, with all malice, be taken away from you. And be* kind one to another, tenderhearted, forgiving one another, just *as God in Christ also forgave you.*"

Ephesians 4: 31-32 (MEV)

DAY 23

Is Your Lamp Lit?

Today, I pray that your walkway will be lit with everything that God has appointed for you to learn. You will get the understanding and knowledge that is needed. You will be afforded the opportunity to walk in a fruitful path set up by Him. The Holy Scriptures are Words of Life with direction. Although, there is correction, the growth that comes from your renewed awareness is light for your path. The Word of God illuminates your path and shines on the dark, hidden agendas of Satan. Yes, you will be surprised how reading the Holy Scriptures at the right time will help you avoid traps that were intended to bring about your demise! Follow the path of the Word. Through your daily reading of the Bible, light will guide your walkway…safely. In Jesus' Name.

PEARL NOTE

"Your Word is a lamp unto my feet and a light to my path."

Psalm 119- 105 (NIV)

DAY 24

Be Encouraged

Today, I pray that you are aware that God has good plans for you. These plans are not for you to self-destruct nor will they allow you to be sabotaged by another. You are good seed, and God thinks the best of you. Let's bring our attention to His plan and see if you are as excited about your future as He is! The negativity of this world will not overcome the knowledge of God concerning the brightness of your future. You will see the good plan that God has for you! In Jesus's Name.

PEARL NOTE

"For I know the plans I have for you," says the Lord. "They are plans for good and not for disaster, to give you a future and a hope."

Jeremiah 29:11 (NLT)

DAY 25

Temptation Is Not From God

Today, I pray that you know you are able to withstand trials and temptations. You desire more than anything to be faithful to God. You have established a relationship that goes beyond doing things to be rewarded by Him. You are in love with Him. You have decided that this is a relationship that is valuable. The temptation is there. But, the desire to be strong in The Lord is greater. It is no secret that you are not being tempted by God. God does not tempt us, especially with evil. Although, there is a great reward of the Crown of Life, you have decided, His will over your appetite. You are blessed with endurance to overcome temptation. In Jesus' Name.

PEARL NOTE

"Blessed is the man who endures temptation; for when he has been approved, he will receive the crown of life which the Lord has promised to those who love Him. Let no one say when he is tempted, 'I am tempted by God'; for God cannot be tempted by evil, nor does He Himself tempt anyone. But each one is tempted when he is drawn away by his own desires and enticed."

James 1: 12-14 (NKJV)

DAY 26

During The Test

Today, I pray that you will know that the plan is still good, in spite of the unexpected mishaps that may appear to be changing the plan. You will maintain the ways that are pleasing to Him, and continue speaking to Him, sincerely, from your heart. You know He is rooting for you, and this too shall pass. It is only a test. So, don't get bent out of shape. You have a firm belief and you are relying on His strength. He knows your recovery is a part of that good plan. You have great expectations even when it looks bad! In Jesus' Name.

PEARL NOTE

"Though He slay me, yet will I trust in Him: but I will maintain mine own ways before Him."

Job 13:15 (KJV)

DAY 27

Check Your Motives

Today, I pray that you examine your motives. You have the ability to ask God to help you discern His ways. It's a possibility that what you take pleasure in is not something that suits the purposes of God for your life. It's important to look into this in order to overcome the ability of losing your way and that which God means for your well-being. The pursuit of your own way can lead to a dead end. Don't deceive yourself. By clinging to God, you will be certain of the course for your life! In Jesus' Name.

PEARL NOTE

> "There is a way that seems right to man, but its end is the way of death."
>
> Proverbs 14:12 (ESV)

DAY 28

Faith And Works

Today, I pray that you take action with works to accomplish what you believe in. Let your faith be activated by your actions. You are fulfilling life through your faith. You have decided to make faith come alive. You will see the powerful combination of faith and works. You are not going to just pray about it, you will become the answer. Someone is observing your belief and your actions will encourage them to do the work, as well. Your faith is not dead! In Jesus' Name.

PEARL NOTE

"What good is it, my brothers and sisters, if someone claims to have faith but has no deeds? Can such faith save them? Suppose a brother or a sister is without clothes and daily food. ¹⁶If one of you says to them, 'Go in peace; keep warm and well fed,' but does nothing about their physical needs, what good is it? ¹In the same way, faith by itself, if it is not accompanied by action, is dead."

James 2: 14-17 (NIV)

DAY 29

Fruit Of Your Lips

Today, I pray that you will speak life over yourself and others. There is a power in your words that can give life, and also cause death. Choose to speak life, to give hope in places where people feel hopeless. You have a tongue that revives and there is someone in need of resuscitation through your words. You have words of color in a world of grey. Speak life without regret. Speak life to cause those that are dying to live. Speak life and restore hope. The power of your tongue will be useful in every way. The power is in your tongue, so use it wisely! In Jesus' Name.

PEARL NOTE

"Words kill, words give life; they're either poison or fruit-you choose."

Proverbs 18:21 (MSG)

DAY 30

Joyous Laughter

Today, I pray that you will laugh with exceeding joy. Your laugh will allow people to see the goodness of God. The presence of your joy will uplift others and bring unity. There are times when laughter comes from a moment of unforgettable elation coming from someone special that you enjoy being around. The joy in your heart brings a merry conversation you can then share with others. This ecstasy comes from God and it supersedes the gloomy places that seek to crowd in on us and rob us of God's precious, comforting gift. Nations are observing your Joy! In Jesus' Name.

PEARL NOTE

"Then our mouth was filled with laughter, and our tongue with shouts of joy; then they said among the nations, The **LORD** *has done great things for them."*

Psalm 126:2 (ESV)

DAY 31

What's Your Contribution?

Today, I pray that you are concerned about your contribution: the investment that you are making into the storehouse designated for you. Are you making a difference for the better? When it is all said and done, don't let your labor be in vain! You are on the go and desire something that is fulfilling; prayerfully, you are putting everything before The Lord. You are making a contribution, and you want to sow into good ground. What a great investment to get involved in praying for others, giving to those in need, and being able to help someone else in whatever way you can! Maybe, it's even an encouraging word that you extend to a hopeless person. You will sow seeds into good ground! In Jesus' Name.

PEARL NOTE

"Be not deceived. God is not mocked. For whatever a man sows that will he also reap."

Galatians 6:7 (MEV)

www.ingramcontent.com/pod-product-compliance
Lightning Source LLC
LaVergne TN
LVHW051508070426
835507LV00022B/2998